100 COCKTAILS

MARTINI
ROSSO
MARTINI
REGISTERED TRADE MARK
VERMOUTH
ROSSO
IMPORTED & BOTTLED BY
MARTINI & ROSSI
LTD
LONDON
NOT LESS THAN 17% VOL
BELLS
Old Scotch
OTHER FAMOUS BELLS
Laurent Perrier
BRUT L.P.
FOURNISSEUR BREVETE
LA COUR DE BELGIQUE
CHAMPAG
urent Pe
COURVOISIER
COGN
40% vol.
16200 JARNAC FRANCE
KIR
Vin Blanc
375 cl

100 COCKTAILS AND DRINKS

Edited by Louise Steele and Wendy James

FANFARE BOOKS

Photographs by Terry Long and Neil Wood

Cover design by James Waugh of Snap Design

This edition published exclusively for Ferroway Limited (Fanfare Books) in 1985 by Orbis Publishing Limited, London

ISBN 0-86370-003-9

Printed in Great Britain.

CONTENTS

INTRODUCTION

Cocktails are more popular today than at any time since their heyday in the 1920s and 1930s. Although there are a thousand and one versions of how cocktails first came into existence and how they were given their name, everyone

seems to agree that they got into their stride during the Prohibition era in the United States. It was an ingenious idea to mix several drinks together, if only to mask the flavour of the poor-quality spirits around at that time! Prohibition was repealed in 1933 and cocktails became respectable, socialites slipping easily into the cocktail habit.

This decade's socialites can choose from an ever-increasing range of spirits, wines and liqueurs, both from home and abroad. You don't need to be a professional bartender to mix a perfect cocktail. All you need are a few basic guidelines to point you in the right direction and a selection of delicious recipes like the ones in this book to send you reaching for the cocktail shaker. Once you've tried and tested all the great classics, and a few of the more modern inventions, no doubt you'll want to think up a few of your own!

THE BAR

Newcomers to the delights of cocktail-making – and drinking! – may well be a little taken aback when faced with the amazing range of spirits, wines, liqueurs and mixers now available. Don't panic! It is, in fact, quite easy to build up a well-stocked cocktail cabinet, starting off with a few basics and gradually acquiring some of the more exotic ingredients, a few at a time.

The five main spirits – whisky, gin, vodka, white rum and brandy – are the essentials on which most recipes are based. Add to these sweet and dry vermouth, Angostura bitters, a few soft drinks such as soda and tonic water, and fruit juices, either freshly-made or ready-pressed, and already you have a host of delicious drinks at your fingertips – try a Sweet or Dry martini, a Manhattan, fruit Daiquiris or a Cuba libre, perhaps. Grenadine, a non-alcoholic pomegranate syrup, is particularly useful for giving drinks a rich red colour – a large part of

the appeal of cocktails lies in their appearance.

Once you have built up your bar stocks – and you may already have many of the ingredients mentioned above in your drinks cabinet – choose from the following which all crop up fairly often: Campari, Galliano, cherry brandy, an orange liqueur (Cointreau, Triple Sec or Curaçao), tequila or dark rum. Sample each new addition as you buy it – not an unpleasant task! – and experiment with the different combinations you can concoct from your store. If you fancy trying out some of the more weird and wonderful drinks on the market, why not buy them in miniature bottles first, to see if you like their flavour? As for buying wines, beers and ciders to make punches and cups, you may find it easier to choose them as and when they are

required, so that you can buy the exact type specified in the recipe.

Although it's generally recommended that you bypass the cheapest and therefore lowest-quality, brands when stocking your bar, don't feel you have to go to the other extreme. There is no need to buy fine wines, champagne brandies or single malt whiskies to make your cocktails with, as their flavour will be masked to some extent when mixed with other drinks. Take care when buying spirits, as mistakes can be expensive. Gin comes in several types: Dutch gin (also called Hollands or Geneva) is probably too highly flavoured to mix in cocktails. Choose either London Dry or Plymouth which are less aromatic. Most Scotch whiskies sold are blended from malt and grain types. Single malts are more expensive. They are usually stronger and are aged for a minimum of seven years, and are an unnecessary extravagance where cocktails are concerned. Don't forget Irish whiskey – usually spelt with an 'e' – which is extremely mellow and mature, and delicious in Irish coffee. Rye and bourbon whiskies are the basis of many classic American cocktails. When buying vodka, give the Polish and Russian varieties a miss – they are much fuller-

flavoured than the almost tasteless modern varieties and quite unsuitable for mixing. Both dark and light rums are useful for the cocktail-maker – dark ones are particularly heart-warming in hot punches, while white rums blend well in long, cooling drinks. Brandies are distilled from grape juice or wine, most being blends. Cognac and Armagnac are made solely in the French districts of the same names. Champagne cognac has no connection with the sparkling wine called champagne – it simply means that the product is made from the finest grapes grown in the best areas within the Cognac district.

Although you may find that the initial outlay for ingredients is rather high, don't forget that you will be using them in smaller quantities, so they'll last much longer.

EQUIPMENT

Although you'll need to make an initial outlay on certain items of equipment, you'll be pleased to know that many basics may already be in your kitchen cupboard, or can be improvised with very little trouble or expense. With the current renewal of interest in cocktails you'll easily be able to find equipment in one of the many specialist shops which have opened up, selling a wide variety of items ranging in quality and price. Many department stores now stock cocktail paraphernalia, too.

The most vital piece of equipment, which lends a professional air to any amateur bartender, is the cocktail shaker. Shakers come in different shapes and sizes, but the classic one consists of three parts – the base, the strainer/cap and the top. Most are made of stainless steel, but you can also buy attractive versions made from reinforced glass. If you're on a tight budget, a screw-top jar, large enough to take all the ingredients including ice, would do the job, although with considerably less style!

If your shaker doesn't have a built-in strainer, you'll need to buy one for transferring the mixtures to the serving glass, leaving behind the ice, bits of fruit and anything else that would spoil the presentation of the drink. Ice is very often added to the shaker, as any left in the cocktail would dilute it. The traditional strainer is also made from stainless steel and is flat, not rounded, with a spring around the edge. At a pinch, a tea-strainer – preferably new, but certainly well-cleaned – could be used.

For drinks which are stirred and not shaken (generally the clear mixtures which don't contain any ingredients like cream or fruit which would make them

cloudy), you'll require a mixing glass, preferably one with a lip to make pouring easier. It should be big enough to hold fairly large capacities: a large tumbler or a beer-mug would both be quite suitable. To mix your drinks you'll also need a long-handled spoon. If you're out to impress your friends, why not buy a muddling spoon? This is a long-handled implement with a spoon at one end, and a 'muddler' at the other. You'll find the latter invaluable for crushing sugar, fruit, mint and so on.

Next on the list of equipment comes a measure. The standard one is 1½ fl oz (4cl) and is also known as a jigger. Double measures can be very handy; they hold a single measure in one side and a double in the other. You probably already have a measuring jug of some description in your kitchen. You could use this or any small container; the most important thing is to measure the ingredients of the cocktail in the correct proportions to each other. Once you're more practised, you can have fun in experimenting to find the proportions to suit your own taste.

A lemon squeezer will be extremely useful for making fresh fruit juices. Freshly-squeezed juice can make a cock-

tail really special. Where some of the more expensive and exotic juices are concerned, however, you may find it cheaper and more convenient to resort to the commercial, ready-squeezed variety. Never substitute squashes for the real thing – they will ruin a drink.

Two essentials which you almost certainly will own already are a corkscrew and a bottle opener. It is well worth investing in the best you can afford – hopefully they will be getting plenty of use! Teaspoons and tablespoons will also be required, as will a sharp knife, a fine grater and a small chopping board for slicing fruit, grating nutmeg and other ingredients, and making garnishes and decorations. Perhaps you have an electric food mixer or blender/liquidizer? These too, will be extremely useful, especially when working with fresh fruit.

Depending on where you usually mix your drinks, you may need an ice bucket and tongs, a glass for hot water in which to rinse your spoons, and a bowl for discarded ice, squeezed fruit and so on. Keep a tea towel or paper towels handy for polishing glasses and mopping up spills. Special hand or mechanical ice crushers are now on the market, but you can easily substitute for them by wrapping ice cubes in a clean tea towel and crushing them with a sturdy rolling pin or mallet.

To serve drinks, you'll obviously need a range of appropriate glasses (see pages 16-19) and a selection of decorations and garnishes (pages 20-1) which go a long way towards the success of your cocktails. Swizzle sticks (for stirring drinks), mats, straws and so on, can turn a simple drink into a spectacular one at very little extra expense.

If you're making a special after-dinner coffee, you'll require a coffee-maker of some sort. Again, there are several types available, including electric filter machines, percolators which sit on the hob or are simply plugged into the power supply, espresso machines, *cafetières* or simple plastic filters which are invaluable for making individual cups of coffee. Don't waste your liqueurs and spirits on instant coffee – it is most definitely a false economy!

Sugar is required for many of the recipes in this book, and the easiest way to use it is in sugar syrup form. In this way, a drink's appearance won't be marred by undissolved crystals floating around in it. To make sugar syrup: put 1 lb (450g) of granulated sugar into a saucepan with 1 pint (560ml) of cold water. Place the pan over a gentle heat till the sugar dissolves, stirring. Boil for 2-3 minutes, remove from the heat and leave to cool. Store in a screw top bottle or jar.

GLASSES

When choosing glasses in which to serve your cocktails, the most important question to ask yourself is 'Will this cocktail look attractive in this particular type of glass?' Appearance is everything. There are no longer any hard and fast rules; just ensure that the glasses are spotlessly clean and that they won't be too unwieldy once they're filled with drink, ice and garnishes.

To clean your glasses, use fresh hot water to which a detergent has been added. Rinse thoroughly to get rid of every last trace of soapsuds – the last flavour you want to incorporate in your drinks is that of washing-up liquid! Leave the glasses to drain, if at all possible. If you need them immediately, polish with a clean linen cloth.

If you store your glasses upside down, remember to 'air' them for at least an hour before use to get rid of the taste of the cupboard and the stale air which has been trapped inside the bowls. Be sure to throw away any cracked or chipped glasses. Apart from the hygiene factor, you risk spoiling the feeling of luxury

you've created for your guests by serving cocktails in chipped glasses!

Here are some general guidelines to the different types of glass available and for which type of drink they are most suitable.

A classic cocktail glass has a long, slim stem to keep the contents cool, and a V-shaped bowl. Glasses of this design can now be found in various sizes, patterns and price ranges, from restrained and elegant to highly patterned, flamboyant and fun. Use this type of glass for cream and fruit cocktails in particular.

The highball is a tall, straight-sided glass which is a perfect container for long drinks loaded with ice or those topped up with soda or mineral water – a Harvey wallbanger or a Pina colada, for example.

A tumbler, or 'old-fashioned', is generally used for spirits or for serving drinks, such as a Bloody Mary, 'on the rocks'.

Wine goblets of all shapes and sizes can be very versatile. Red wines (and therefore red-wine based cocktails) are traditionally served at room temperature in a rounded Paris goblet, which allows the wine to breathe, whilst white wines are served chilled in a tulip – a taller, slimmer, slightly longer-stemmed glass.

Champagne is generally served in either a *flûte* or a champagne saucer. The *flûte* is, in fact, the correct choice, as a saucer, though glamorous, allows the bubbles in the wine to escape much too quickly. Cocktails made with sparkling wines may be served successfully in either type of glass.

Smaller cocktails are happier in smaller glasses, the port, sherry or liqueur types all being suitable. Tall Pilsner glasses are equally good for serving beer-based drinks or some of the more exotic cocktails, while tankards are only really suitable for beer and drinks like Black velvet. Brandy balloons can make spectacular containers, but aren't really suitable for drinks which must be kept well chilled, as their shape dictates that they are held cupped in the hand.

If you enjoy making punches and cups, you may wish to consider investing in a punch bowl with matching cups and serving spoon or ladle. It makes an excellent centrepiece at parties.

Liqueur coffees can either be served in *demi-tasse* size cups, tumblers or wine goblets. Clear containers show the different layers formed when you've floated cream on top of the coffee – very impressive, but only use them if you've perfected this particular art! Arrange a few chocolates or mints on a pretty dish to accompany the coffee, and you have a delicious finish to any meal.

GARNISHES

Cocktail garnishes have come a long way since the days of the single cherry or olive. Here is the opportunity to let your imagination run riot. Be careful not to overwhelm your cocktail, however. No-one wants to have to plough their way through a jungle of paper parasols, fresh fruit, plastic animals or even fireworks to get down to the serious business!

Although garnishes can usually be varied according to taste and availability, in a few cases they form an essential part of a recipe. A Dry martini without its olive, or a Pimm's without its cucumber would be unthinkable! The secret is to marry the colour and flavour of a garnish to the ingredients of the cocktail. Thus slices of fresh pineapple with a Pina colada or fresh lime or lemon with a Margarita are obvious choices.

Fresh fruit is the most frequently used cocktail garnish. Be imaginative with it – use the peel, make twists, slice it, make segments or butterflies, or combine two or three different fruits for the same drink. Tinned fruit is no real substitute – it is sweet and syrupy and nowhere near as firm as its fresh equivalent. Experiment with attractive and unusual fruits, such as guava, papaya and kiwifruit. Other edible garnishes include grated spices, coconut, mint, almonds and olives too, of course.

You will probably come across a fascinating range of cocktail paraphernalia when browsing in specialist shops. Paper parasols, weird and wonderful straws, coloured stirrers and mats, ice cubes in fun shapes – just take your pick!

A very simple but effective way of decorating glasses is to frost the rim. Rub it lightly with a cut lemon and dip it into fine caster sugar or salt. Tap the glass to remove the excess, and leave it to set for a few minutes before pouring in the cocktail.

PUNCHES & CUPS

Planters' punch

Overall timing 5–7 minutes plus cooling

To serve 4

4 tbsp (4×15 ml) Caster sugar
4 tbsp (4×15 ml) Water
8 tbsp (8×15 ml) Lime juice
12fl oz (240 ml) Dark Jamaica rum
3–4 Drops Angostura bitters
Ice cubes
1 Sliced lime
1 Sliced lemon
1 Sliced orange

Heat the sugar and water in a small pan till sugar dissolves, stirring. Leave to cool.

• Pour into a cocktail shaker and add the lime juice, rum and Angostura. Shake vigorously.

• Place ice cubes in a large jug and pour over punch. Add slices of citrus fruit and serve.

Lychee punch bowl

Overall timing 5 minutes plus chilling

To serve 8

2×16 oz (2×454 g) Cans of lychees	
Juice of ½ lemon	
1 tbsp (15 ml) Maraschino	
¼ pint (150 ml) Dry sherry	
2 Bottles of dry white wine	
1¼ pints (700 ml) Dry cider	
Ice cubes	

Drain lychees and put into a punch bowl with the lemon juice, Maraschino, sherry and half the wine. Chill for 2 hours.

• Add remaining wine and cider and serve immediately with ice cubes.

Créole punch

Overall timing 5 minutes plus preparing sugar syrup (see page 15), frosting glasses and cooling

To serve 4

Ice cubes

4 tbsp (4×15 ml) Sugar syrup (see page 2)

8 tbsp (8×15 ml) White rum

4 tbsp (4×15 ml) Lime juice

4 Strips of lime rind

Lemonade

Frost the rims of 4 chilled glasses with sugar.

• Put an ice cube in each glass and divide syrup, rum and lime juice between them.

• Add a strip of lime rind to each and top up with lemonade. Decorate with extra lime rind if liked and serve with a straw.

Peach punch

Overall timing 15 minutes plus chilling

To serve 10–12

1 Bottle of peach wine
2 Bottles of sparkling dry white wine
1 lb (450 g) Yellow peaches
1 Orange
2 Lemons
½ pint (300 ml) Cognac or Grand Marnier
1 pint (560 ml) Soda water
Ice cubes

Chill bottles of wine. Meanwhile, peel, halve and finely chop peaches. Place in jug or punch bowl with peeled and thinly sliced orange, juice from the lemons and Cognac or Grand Marnier. Place in fridge for 1 hour.
● Just before serving, add ice cubes to jug or punch bowl and pour in the peach and sparkling wines, and soda water.

Sauternes punch

Overall timing
5 minutes

To serve 8

2 Bottles of chilled Sauternes
1fl oz (30 ml) Maraschino
1fl oz (30 ml) Curaçao
1fl oz (30 ml) Grand Marnier
Seasonal fruits

Place chilled bottles of Sauternes in a large jug or punch bowl together with the Maraschino, Curaçao and Grand Marnier.

• Add a selection of seasonal fruits and stir well before serving.

Rhine wine punch

Overall timing
15 minutes

To serve 18–20

6 pints (3.5 litres) Chilled Rhine wine
1 pint (560 ml) Chilled sparkling mineral water
2fl oz (60 ml) Brandy
2fl oz (60 ml) Maraschino
8 oz (225 g) Icing sugar
2 tbsp (2×15 ml) Tea leaves

Place the wine and mineral water in a large punch bowl with the brandy, Maraschino and icing sugar.
- Add the tea leaves, tied in a piece of muslin, and leave to infuse for 10 minutes.
- Remove the tea from punch and stir well before serving.

Hallowe'en punch

Overall timing 50 minutes, plus chilling

To serve 8

1 lb (450 g) Pumpkin flesh
1 pint (560 ml) Water
3 oz (75 g) Sugar
3 inch (7.6 cm) Piece of cinnamon stick
1 pint (560 ml) Orange juice
3 pints (1.7 litres) Sparkling cider
1 Orange

• Chop pumpkin flesh and place in a pan with water, sugar and cinnamon. Heat gently, stirring, till sugar dissolves. Bring to boil and simmer for 20 minutes till pumpkin is tender. Discard cinnamon,

• purée rest in a blender or rub through a sieve into a bowl. Mix in orange juice, then chill for 3–4 hours. Chill the cider and add to bowl with sliced orange.

Cold beer punch

Overall timing 35 minutes plus cooling

To serve 4–6

½ pint (300 ml) Water
4 oz (125 g) Sugar
1 Lemon
6 Cloves
¼ pint (150 ml) Grapefruit juice
½ pint (300 ml) Lemon juice
10–15 Ice cubes
¾ pint (400 ml) Light ale
Thin slices of lemon
Sprigs of mint

Heat the water and sugar in a saucepan till sugar dissolves. Pare rind thinly from lemon and add to pan with cloves. Cover and simmer for 30 minutes.

• Remove rind and cloves and leave to cool.

• Add fruit juices and strain mixture into a punch bowl. Add ice cubes and light ale. Float mint and lemon slices on top of punch.

Hot beer punch

Overall timing
10 minutes

To serve 4–6

4 Eggs, separated
4 teasp (4×5 ml) Caster sugar
4 teasp (4×5 ml) Lemon juice
2 pints (1.1 litres) Light ale
2 Strips of lemon rind
Grated nutmeg

Stiffly whisk egg whites then whisk in the caster sugar.

• Mix egg yolks and lemon juice. Heat light ale in a saucepan with lemon rind (do not boil). Remove rind and discard.

• Pour light ale on to egg yolks and lemon juice and mix well. Divide egg whites between tall glasses, then pour in the beer and egg mixture. Stir gently and sprinkle with grated nutmeg.

Champagne cup

Overall timing
5 minutes

To serve 6

1 Bottle of chilled Champagne
2fl oz (60 ml) Brandy
2fl oz (60 ml) Curaçao
1fl oz (30 ml) Maraschino
1fl oz (30 ml) Grand Marnier
2 teasp (2×5 ml) Icing sugar
Ice cubes
1 Sliced orange
6 Strawberries

Place chilled Champagne, Brandy, Curaçao, Maraschino and Grand Marnier in a punch bowl or large jug.

• Add the icing sugar and ice cubes and stir well.

• Serve over ice in glasses, decorated with orange slices and strawberries.

Peaches and wine

Overall timing
7 minutes plus maceration

To serve 10–12

- 3 Ripe peaches or 14 oz (400 g) Can of sliced peaches
- 1 Bottle of chilled still Moselle
- 1 Bottle of chilled sparkling Moselle
- 1–2 tbsp (15–30 ml) Caster sugar

Peel, stone and chop the fresh peaches, or drain and chop the canned peaches if using. Place fruit in a large punch bowl or jug.

• Add ½ the bottle of still Moselle and leave to macerate for 20–30 minutes.

• Stir in the remaining chilled still wine, the sparkling wine and the sugar. Stir lightly and serve.

Rhine wine cup

Overall timing
5 minutes

To serve 4–6

1 Bottle of chilled Rhine wine
1fl oz (30 ml) Curaçao
2fl oz (60 ml) Maraschino
1 teasp (5 ml) Icing sugar
4–5 Ice cubes
Pineapple pieces
Orange slices

Place the chilled wine, Curaçao, Maraschino and icing sugar in a large jug. Add the ice cubes and stir well.

- Serve in glasses, decorated with pieces of pineapple and orange slices.

Bubbly cup

Overall timing
7 minutes plus chilling

To serve 8–10

1 Sliced lemon
2 Sprigs of borage
1 tbsp (15 ml) Caster sugar
¾ pint (450 ml) Dry sherry
1 Bottle chilled hock
18fl oz (500 ml) Bottle chilled soda water

Put the slices of lemon into a punch bowl. Wash and dry the sprigs of borage and add to lemon slices with the caster sugar.

- Stir in dry sherry and place in fridge for 2 hours.
- Just before serving mix in the chilled hock and soda water. Ladle into tall chilled glasses.

Strawberry red wine cup

Overall timing 10 minutes plus maceration

To serve 8

1 lb (450 g) Small ripe strawberries
4 tbsp (4×15 ml) Icing sugar
2 Large oranges
1 Large bottle chilled Beaujolais
8 Frozen orange slices

Hull the strawberries and put into a tall jug with the icing sugar and juice squeezed from oranges. Mix lightly and leave to macerate in the fridge for 1 hour.

• Add Beaujolais, mix lightly and serve in chilled glasses. Add a frozen orange slice to each glass just before serving.

Claret cup

Overall timing
5 minutes

To serve 4–6

6 Ice cubes
1 Bottle of claret
2fl oz (60 ml) Maraschino
1½fl oz (40 ml) Curaçao
2 teasp (2×5 ml) Icing sugar
1 Sliced orange
1 Sliced red apple

Place the ice cubes and claret in a large jug.
• Stir in the Maraschino, Curaçao and icing sugar and mix well until thoroughly combined.
• Decorate with orange and apple slices before serving.

Claret refresher

Overall timing
5 minutes

To serve 3–4

4–5 Ice cubes
3/4 pint (450 ml) Claret
1/2 pint (300 ml) Lemon juice
Soda water

Crack the ice cubes and place in a shaker with the claret and lemon juice.
• Shake vigorously until thoroughly combined then strain into large glasses and top up with soda water to taste.

Sangria

Overall timing
5 minutes

To serve 8–10

1 Bottle red wine
4fl oz (120 ml) Brandy
12fl oz (350 ml) Fizzy lemonade
8 Ice cubes
1 Sliced orange
1 Sliced lemon
1 Sliced lime

Put the red wine, brandy and chilled lemonade in a large jug or punch bowl. Add the ice cubes and pour into glasses.

• Spear the sliced fruits on to cocktail sticks and use to decorate each glass.

White wine and Cointreau

Overall timing
3–5 minutes

To serve 2–3

½ pint (300 ml) Chilled dry white wine
2½fl oz (65 ml) Cointreau
3 Ice cubes
½ pint (300 ml) Chilled soda water
Orange slices

Place the chilled wine, Cointreau and ice cubes in a mixing glass, stir well and strain into 2 or 3 glasses.

• Top up each one with chilled soda water and decorate with orange slices.

Red wine cooler

Overall timing
5 minutes plus preparing sugar syrup (see page 15)

To serve 4–6

- 12 Ice cubes
- 1 pint (560 ml) Red wine
- ¼ pint (150 ml) White rum
- 2½fl oz (65 ml) Sugar syrup (see page 15)
- 2 tbsp (2×15 ml) Orange juice (unsweetened)
- 2 tbsp (2×15 ml) Lemon juice
- Soda water
- 4–6 Lemon slices

Place the ice cubes and all other ingredients, except the soda water and lemon slices, in a jug and mix well.

• Pour into 4–6 tall glasses or tumblers. Top up with soda water to taste and decorate each glass with a slice of lemon.

Caribbean cooler

Overall timing
5 minutes

To serve 8

3 Limes
½ pint (300 ml) Sugar syrup (see page 15)
8 tbsp (8×15 ml) Dark rum
8 Orange slices
8 Ice cubes
Ginger ale

Pare 8 thin strips of rind from the limes and reserve. Squeeze out the juice and pour into a large jug, add the sugar syrup and rum and mix well.

- Divide rum mixture between glasses. Add a slice of orange to each.
- Crush ice cubes. Divide between glasses and top up with ginger ale.
- Add strips of lemon rind and serve with straws.

Cider fizz

Overall timing 2 hours

To serve 8

- 4 Oranges
- 4 lemons
- 1¾ pints (1 litre) Sparkling cider
- 12 oz (350 g) Caster sugar
- 6 tbsp (6×15 ml) Rum
- 1 tbsp (15 ml) Water
- 3 Egg whites
- Salt
- 2 tbsp (2×15 ml) Icing sugar

Squeeze juice from fruit and strain into a jug.
- Heat cider and the caster sugar in a saucepan over gentle heat, stirring, for 6–7 minutes till sugar dissolves, then simmer. Skim surface. Cool quickly. Add to fruit juices in a jug with rum and chill for 1 hour.
- Beat water and egg whites with a pinch of salt till stiff, then beat in icing sugar. Pour fruit syrup into egg whites, then pour back into jug.

Winter warmer

Overall timing
20 minutes

To serve 4–6

- 1 Bottle of red wine
- 2fl oz (60 ml) Orange juice (unsweetened)
- 4fl oz (120 ml) Port
- 2fl oz (60 ml) Brandy
- 2 tbsp (2×15 ml) Caster sugar
- 10 Whole cloves
- 2 Cinnamon sticks

Place all the ingredients in a saucepan and heat through gently for 15 minutes, stirring occasionally. (Do not allow to boil.)

• Ladle into heatproof glasses and serve hot.

Cognac and lemon punch

Overall timing
10 minutes

To serve 6–8

1¾ pints (1 litre) Sweet white wine
2 Lemons
8 oz (225 g) Caster sugar
2 Cloves
¼ pint (150 ml) Cognac
Lemon slices

Put the sweet white wine into a saucepan with the finely grated rinds of 2 lemons, the sugar and cloves. Heat gently till the sugar dissolves.

• Warm the Cognac in a small pan, add to the wine and set alight. When the flames have died down, strain into a heatproof jug.

• Garnish with slices of lemon and serve immediately in heatproof glasses.

Hot apple punch

Overall timing
45–50 minutes

To serve 8–10

3 Dessert apples
2 tbsp (2×15 ml) Caster sugar
1¾ pints (1 litre) Full-bodied red wine
2 oz (50 g) Sugar lumps
1 Lemon spiked with 2 cloves

Slice apples thickly into a flameproof dish. Sprinkle with caster sugar and grill for about 5 minutes till golden.

• Put the red wine into a saucepan with the sugar lumps and the lemon. Heat gently till a scum forms. Add the apples and remove from heat.

• Cover and leave to infuse for 30 minutes.

• Discard lemon and purée mixture in a blender. Reheat gently and pour into a heatproof jug or bowl.

Bischof

Overall timing
15 minutes plus overnight maceration

To serve 6–8

2 Large oranges
1¾ pints (1 litre) White wine
2 inch (5cm) Piece of cinnamon stick
6 oz (175 g) Caster sugar

Wash 2 large oranges and pare off the rind in strips using a potato peeler. Put into a large jug with the white wine, cinnamon stick and caster sugar. Mix well and leave to macerate overnight.

- The next day, pour into a large saucepan and heat till almost boiling. Strain into a heatproof bowl or jug. Pour or ladle into heatproof glasses.

Orange grog

Overall timing
7–10 minutes

To serve 4

3 Oranges
½ pint (300 ml) Water
4 oz (125 g) Caster sugar
8 tbsp (8×15 ml) Dark rum

Wash the oranges. Pare the rind and then squeeze the juice from 2 and slice the third one thinly.

• Put the water into a saucepan with the pared rind and caster sugar and heat gently till the sugar dissolves. Add the orange juice and remove from the heat.

• Put 2 tbsp (2×15 ml) dark rum into each of 4 heatproof glasses and strain the orange syrup on to the rum. Serve immediately.

COCKTAILS & LIQUEURS

Sherry and vermouth

Overall timing
3 minutes

To serve 2

2–3 Ice cubes
¼ pint (150 ml) Dry sherry
2½fl oz (65 ml) Sweet vermouth
2 Dashes Angostura bitters
Seasonal fruits (optional)

Place the ice cubes, sherry, vermouth and Angostura bitters in a mixing glass and stir well.
• Strain into wine glasses and serve decorated with seasonal fruits, if liked.

Manhattan cocktail

Overall timing
3–5 minutes

To serve 1

2–3 Ice cubes
½fl oz (15 ml) Dry vermouth
½fl oz (15 ml) Sweet vermouth
1fl oz (25 ml) Whisky
1 Strawberry or olive

Crack the ice and place in a shaker together with the dry and sweet vermouths and whisky.
• Shake vigorously until thoroughly blended then strain into a glass and decorate with a strawberry or an olive, as liked.

Bloody Mary

Overall timing
5 minutes

To serve 4

12fl oz (350 ml) Chilled tomato juice
1 teasp (5 ml) Lemon juice
6fl oz (170 ml) Vodka
2 teasp (2×5 ml) Worcester sauce
¼ teasp (1.25 ml) Celery salt
2–3 Drops of Tabasco sauce
8–12 Ice cubes

In a large jug put the chilled tomato juice, lemon juice, vodka, Worcester sauce, celery salt, pepper and Tabasco sauce.
• Stir ingredients together well. Put 2–3 ice cubes in each glass and pour in the vodka mixture. Serve immediately.

Dry martini

Overall timing
2–3 minutes

To serve 4
Crushed ice
1½fl oz (45 ml) Dry vermouth
9fl oz (250 ml) Dry gin
Strips of lemon peel or
1–2 Dashes of bitters
4 Olives

In a large jug put some crushed ice and the dry vermouth and gin. Stir very, very well.
• Strain liquor into glasses and either twist strips of lemon peel over each glass or add 1–2 dashes of bitters.
• To each glass, add an olive on cocktail stick.

Medium martini

Overall timing
3 minutes

To serve 1

2–3 Ice cubes
½fl oz (15 ml) Dry vermouth
½fl oz (15 ml) Sweet vermouth
1fl oz (25 ml) Gin
1 Maraschino cherry

Crack the ice cubes and place in a shaker together with the dry and sweet vermouths and the gin.
• Shake vigorously until thoroughly blended then strain into a glass and decorate with maraschino cherry.

Rose cocktail

Overall timing
2–3 minutes

To serve 4

6fl oz (170 ml) Dry vermouth
2fl oz (60 ml) Kirsch
1 tbsp (15 ml) Raspberry syrup
8–12 Ice cubes
4 Maraschino cherries

In a large jug put the dry vermouth, Kirsch and raspberry syrup. Stir well.
• Put 2–3 ice cubes in each glass and pour over the rose cocktail.
• Serve with a maraschino cherry in each glass.

Gin fizz

Overall timing
2–3 minutes plus preparing sugar syrup (see page 15) and frosting glasses

To serve 4

Crushed ice
2 tbsp (2×15 ml) Sugar syrup (see recipe, page 15)
4fl oz (120 ml) Gin
2 Lemons
Soda water

In a shaker put some crushed ice and add the sugar syrup, gin and juice of the lemons. Shake vigorously.

• Frost the rims of 4 tall glasses with sugar.

• Strain the cocktail into prepared glasses and top up with the soda water, stirring all the time as it is added.

Variation

• For Crimson fizz, add 6–8 crushed strawberries to the other ingredients in the shaker.

Colonel Collins

Overall timing
2–3 minutes plus preparing sugar syrup (see page 15)

To serve 4

4 tbsp (4×15 ml) Sugar syrup (see recipe, page 15)
4 Lemons
4fl oz (90 ml) Bourbon whiskey
8–12 Ice cubes
Soda water
4 Slices of lemon

In a large jug put sugar syrup, the juice of 4 lemons and Bourbon. Mix well.

- Put 2–3 ice cubes into 4 tall glasses. Pour in cocktail and top up with soda water, stirring all the time.
- Decorate with a slice of lemon on the side of each glass. Serve with a straw.

Variation

- For a John Collins, substitute dry gin for Bourbon.

Pimm's

Overall timing
2–3 minutes

To serve 1

- 1 Slice of cucumber or piece of cucumber rind
- 1 Slice of lemon or
- 1 Slice of apple or orange (or all)
- Ice cubes
- Sprig of borage or mint
- 2fl oz (60 ml) Pimm's No. 1
- 1fl oz (30 ml) Gin or Cointreau (optional)
- Lemonade

Put the slice of cucumber, or rind, lemon, apple or orange slice (or all) into a ½ pint tankard. Add ice and the sprig of borage or mint.

- Add Pimm's No. 1, gin or Cointreau if using and top up with lemonade.

Champagne cocktail

Overall timing
2–3 minutes

To serve 1

½ teasp (2.5 ml) Sugar syrup (see page 15)
1 tbsp (15 ml) Well-chilled brandy
Chilled dry Champagne
¼ teasp (1.25 ml) Yellow Chartreuse or Curaçao
2–3 Drops of Angostura bitters
1 Slice of lemon

Into a champagne glass put the sugar syrup and brandy. Fill almost to the top of glass with chilled Champagne.
• Add the Chartreuse or Curaçao and Angostura bitters. Stir and decorate with a slice of lemon on the side of the glass.

Variation
• Place a lump of sugar in the glass, add a few shakes of Angostura bitters and decorate with a slice of orange.

Gimlet

Overall timing
2–3 minutes plus preparing sugar syrup (see page 15)

To serve 4

Crushed ice
1 tbsp (15 ml) Sugar syrup (see page 15)
4fl oz (120 ml) Fresh lime juice
8fl oz (220 ml) Gin

In a shaker put some crushed ice, the sugar syrup, lime juice and gin.
• Shake vigorously, then strain into 4 chilled glasses.

Variation
• For Orange blossom, substitute fresh orange juice for half the lime juice. Also vodka can be used instead of gin.

Daiquiri

Overall timing
2–3 minutes plus preparing sugar syrup (see page 15)

To serve 4

Crushed ice
1 tbsp (15 ml) Sugar syrup (see page 15)
2fl oz (60 ml) Lime juice
½ pint (300 ml) White rum

In a shaker put some crushed ice and add the sugar syrup, lime juice and white rum.

• Shake vigorously and then strain into 4 chilled glasses.

• Variations

• For Pink daiquiri, substitute 1 tbsp (15 ml) grenadine syrup for the sugar syrup. For Golden glove, add 1 teasp (5 ml) Cointreau to basic mixture. Or add 1 teasp (5 ml) orange juice and ¼ teasp (1.25 ml) Curaçao to each drink.

Margarita

Overall timing
2–3 minutes plus frosting the glasses

To serve 4

8fl oz (220 ml) Tequila
4fl oz (120 ml) Fresh lime or lemon juice
1 tbsp (15 ml) Cointreau or Triple Sec
Ice cubes

In a large jug put the tequila, lime or lemon juice and Cointreau or Triple Sec.
- Add the ice cubes and stir well.
- Frost the rims of glasses with salt and shake off the excess.
- Pour in the tequila mixture and serve immediately.

Americano

Overall timing
3–4 minutes plus frosting glasses

To serve 4

1 Sliced orange
1 Sliced lemon
Ice cubes
6fl oz (170 ml) Campari
12fl oz (350 ml) Red vermouth
1 teasp (5 ml) Dry white vermouth
Soda water

In a large jug put the sliced orange and lemon and ice cubes. Add Campari, red vermouth and white vermouth. Mix well.

• Put 2–3 ice cubes into chilled, frosted (with sugar) glasses and pour in the cocktail.

• Top up with soda water to taste and decorate with a slice of orange on each glass.

Cuba libre

Overall timing
5 minutes

To serve 4

8fl oz (220 ml) White rum
4 tbsp (4×15 ml) Fresh lime juice
8–12 Ice cubes
Cola
4 Twists of lime or lemon

In a jug mix together the white rum and lime juice.
• Put 2–3 ice cubes in each glass. Pour in the rum mixture to half-fill and then top up with cola.
• Serve with a twist of lime or lemon and a straw if liked.

Negroni

Overall timing
2–3 minutes

To serve 4
8fl oz (220 ml) Dry gin
4fl oz (120 ml) Sweet vermouth
4fl oz (120ml) Campari
8–12 Ice cubes

In a jug mix together the dry gin, sweet vermouth and Campari.
• Put 2–3 ice cubes in each glass and pour over the cocktail. Serve immediately.

Vermouth cocktail

Overall timing
3 minutes

To serve 1

2–3 Ice cubes
2fl oz (50 ml) Dry or sweet vermouth
3–4 Dashes orange bitters
1–2 Dashes Angostura bitters
1 Strip of orange peel

Place the ice cubes in a mixing glass. Add the vermouth, orange bitters and Angostura.

• Stir well then strain into a glass and decorate with a strip of orange peel.

Advocaat

Overall timing
15 minutes plus cooling

To serve 4

3 Egg yolks
½–1 oz (15–25 g) Caster sugar
6fl oz (170 ml) Brandy
Vanilla essence
Ice cubes

Put egg yolks and sugar in a bowl. Place over a pan of hot water and whisk until the mixture is thick, creamy and doubled in volume.

• Remove the bowl from heat and continue whisking until mixture is cool.

• Stir in the brandy and vanilla essence to taste.

• Pour advocaat into 4 glasses, add ice cubes and straws and serve.

Variation

• Instead of brandy, use any fruit brandy (for example, cherry, peach or apricot).

Creole eggnog

Overall timing
10 minutes

To serve 6

3 Eggs
14 oz (397 g) Can of condensed milk
Grated rind of a lemon
Angostura bitters
½ pint (300 ml) Trinidad rum
6 Ice cubes
Lemon slices
Cocktail cherries

Lightly beat the eggs in a bowl, then beat in the condensed milk. Add the lemon rind and a few drops of Angostura bitters and whisk in the rum.

• Crush the ice and divide between punch cups or glasses. Pour the egg mixture over. Decorate with lemon slices and cocktail cherries and serve.

Harvey Wallbanger

Overall timing
1–2 minutes

To serve 1
1 Measure of vodka
4 Measures of fresh orange juice
Ice cubes
½ Measure of Liquore Galliano
½ Slice of lemon

Put vodka, orange juice and plenty of ice cubes into a tall glass. Stir well.
• Add Liquore Galliano, and serve with a half slice of lemon.

Sidecar

Overall timing
3–4 minutes

To serve 4–6

Crushed ice
1 Measure Cointreau or Triple Sec
2 Measures lemon juice
8 Measures Cognac or brandy

In a shaker, put some crushed ice, the Cointreau or Triple Sec, lemon juice and Cognac or brandy.
• Shake vigorously then strain into glasses.

• **Variation**
• To make a Knight, put some crushed ice in a shaker with 1 measure mixed Cointreau and Chartreuse, 2 measures lemon juice and 8 measures Cognac or brandy. Shake well and strain into glasses.

Miami

Overall timing
3–4 minutes plus frosting glasses

To serve 4–6

1 Measure white Crème de Menthe
2 Measures lemon or lime juice
8 Measures white rum
Crushed ice

In a shaker, put the Crème de Menthe, lemon or lime juice and white rum. Add crushed ice and shake vigorously.

• Frost the rims of 4 glasses with sugar. Pour cocktail into glasses and serve.

White lady

Overall timing
2–3 minutes plus frosting glasses

To serve 4

Crushed ice
2 Measures gin
2 Measures Cointreau
3 Measures lemon juice
4 Cherries

In a shaker, put some crushed ice, the gin, Cointreau and lemon juice.

• Shake vigorously and pour into (sugar) frosted glasses. Add a cherry to each one and serve.

Aviation

Overall timing
2–3 minutes

To serve 4–6

Crushed ice
1 Measure Maraschino
2 Measures lemon juice
8 Measures Gin

In a shaker, put some crushed ice and add the Maraschino, lemon juice and gin.
• Shake vigorously and then pour into glasses and serve.

Greenback

Overall timing
2–3 minutes

To serve 4

1 Measure green Crème de menthe
2 Measures strained lime juice
8 Measures gin
Ice cubes

In a jug, put the Crème de Menthe, strained lime juice and gin. Add ice cubes and stir well.

• Pour into glasses and serve.

Curaçao

Overall timing
3–4 minutes

To serve 4–6

Crushed ice
2 Measures Curaçao
1 Measure lemon juice
6 Measures whisky
4–6 Twists of lemon rind

In a shaker or jug, put some crushed ice. Add the Curaçao, lemon juice and whisky.

- Shake or stir well and pour into glasses. Serve each one with a twist of lemon rind.

Frisco

Overall timing
2–3 minutes

To serve 4–6

Cracked ice
2 Measures Bénédictine
1 Measure lemon juice
6 Measures whisky

In a shaker or jug, put some cracked ice. Add the Bénédictine, lemon juice and whisky.

• Shake or stir well and pour into glasses.

Panama

Overall timing
3–4 minutes

To serve 4
Crushed ice
1 Measure sweetened single cream
1 Measure Crème de Cacao
3–4 Measures Cognac

In a shaker, put some crushed ice and add sweetened single cream, Crème de Cacao and Cognac.
• Shake vigorously and pour into glasses.

Kir

Overall timing 1 minute

To serve 1

Crème de Cassis or blackcurrant syrup

Chilled dry white wine

Place Crème de Cassis to taste (or blackcurrant syrup, if using) in a glass.

• Top up with chilled white wine to taste.

Pina colada

Overall timing
1–2 minutes

To serve 6

3/4 pint (400 ml) Unsweetened pineapple juice or
15½ oz (439 g) Can crushed pineapple (drained)
7fl oz (200 ml) Canned coconut milk
7fl oz (200 ml) White rum (Bacardi)
6–8 Ice cubes
6 Maraschino cherries
6 Thin rings of fresh pineapple

Put in a blender the pineapple juice or drained, crushed pineapple. Add the coconut milk, rum and ice cubes.

- Blend for 15–20 seconds, then pour into tall, chilled glasses.
- Decorate each one with a Maraschino cherry and pineapple ring.

Claret flip

Overall timing
3 minutes plus preparing sugar syrup (see page 15)

To serve 1
2–3 Ice cubes
3fl oz (85 ml) Red wine
1 Egg yolk
2 teasp (2×5 ml) Sugar syrup (see page 15)

Crack the ice cubes and place in a shaker together with the wine, egg yolk and sugar syrup.
• Shake vigorously until thoroughly blended then strain into a glass.

Black velvet

Overall timing
2 minutes

To serve 1

¼ pint (150 ml) Guinness
¼ pint (150 ml) Champagne

Carefully pour the chilled Guinness and chilled Champagne together into a tall glass, tumbler or tankard. Serve immediately.

Buck's fizz

Overall timing
2 minutes

To serve 2–3

1/4 pint (150 ml) Orange juice (unsweetened)
1/2 pint (300 ml) Champagne

Pour the chilled orange juice into 2 or 3 glasses or flûtes.
• Top up carefully with the chilled Champagne. Serve immediately.

Port refresher

Overall timing 2–3 minutes

To serve 2

- 2–3 Ice cubes
- ¼ pint (150 ml) Port
- 2½fl oz (65 ml) Cointreau
- 1 teasp (5 ml) Icing or caster sugar
- 4 Olives
- 2 Cucumber slices

Crack the ice cubes and put into a shaker with the port, Cointreau and sugar.

• Shake vigorously until thoroughly blended then strain into glasses.

• Decorate each one with a cocktail stick speared with 2 olives and a cucumber slice.

Port flip

Overall timing
2–3 minutes

To serve 1
2–3 Ice cubes
2½fl oz (65 ml) Port
1 Egg
2 teasp (2×5 ml) Icing or caster sugar
Ground nutmeg

Crack the ice cubes and put into a shaker with the port, egg and sugar. Shake vigorously until thoroughly combined • then strain into a glass and add 1 or 2 pinches of nutmeg to taste.

Port wine cocktail

Overall timing
2–3 minutes

To serve 1
2–3 Ice cubes
2½fl oz (65 ml) Port
1 Dash Angostura
1 Dash orange bitters
3 Dashes Curaçao

Place the ice cubes in a mixing glass together with the port, Angostura, orange bitters and Curaçao.

• Stir well and strain into a glass.

Madeira sangaree

Overall timing
2–3 minutes

To serve 1
2–3 Ice cubes
¼ pint (150 ml) Madeira
1 teasp (5 ml) Icing sugar

Place the ice cubes in a wine glass.
• Add the Madeira and icing sugar and stir thoroughly until combined before serving.

Sherry refresher

Overall timing
3 minutes plus preparing sugar syrup (see page 15)

To serve 1

4 Ice cubes
2 Orange slices
1 Lemon slice
¼ pint (150 ml) Dry sherry
1fl oz (30 ml) Sugar syrup (see page 15)

Place the crushed ice cubes and slices of orange and lemon in a tall tumbler.

• Add the sherry and sugar syrup and stir thoroughly until combined before serving.

Minted gin tea

Overall timing
7–10 minutes

To serve 4

2 teasp (2×5 ml) Tea leaves
2 teasp (2×5 ml) Fresh chopped mint
3/4 pint (400 ml) Boiling water
1 Lime or
1/2 lemon
4 tbsp (4×15 ml) Gin
Ice cubes

Put tea leaves and chopped mint into a teapot and pour over boiling water. Leave to infuse for 5 minutes, then strain. Leave till cold.

- Pare the rind from the lime or lemon and reserve. Squeeze out the juice from fruit. Add to the tea with gin.
- Frost the rims of 4 tall glasses with sugar. Pour in the minted tea and serve with ice and reserved rind.

Loganberry cordial

Overall timing 20 minutes plus maceration

Makes 1¾ pints (1 litre)

1 lb (450 g) Loganberries
1¼ pints (700 ml) Dry white wine
2½ lb (1.1 kg) Caster sugar

Place prepared loganberries in a bowl with the wine and leave in the fridge for 3 hours.

• Strain loganberries through a sieve into a pan, pressing them with a wooden spoon. Place pan over gentle heat, add sugar and stir constantly till it dissolves. Bring to the boil slowly, then remove from heat.

• Strain liquid through muslin. Pour into warmed bottles and cork, making sure bottles are airtight. Store in a cool, dark place.

• Serve with ice and water or soda water.

Apricot kernel liqueur

Overall timing 45 minutes plus maturing

Makes 2½ pints (1.5 litres)

- 1 lb (450 g) Apricot stones
- 1¼ lb (600 g) Cube sugar
- 1¾ pints (1 litre) Gin or vodka
- 3fl oz (90 ml) Cognac

Crush 10 of the apricot stones and put the kernels and shells into a wide-necked, airtight jar.

- Crack the remaining stones, remove the kernels and skin them. Place kernels in jar with the sugar, then cover with spirit. Cover the jar.
- Leave for 3–4 months to mature, shaking the jar once a week.
- Strain the liqueur through muslin and add the Cognac. Put into sterilized bottles and seal tighly. Leave for 2 more months before drinking.

Hangman's liqueur

Overall timing 20 minutes plus maturing

Makes 2 pints (1.1 litre)

1¾ pints (1 litre) Gin or vodka

14 oz (400 g) Caster sugar

1 Large fresh orange

Put the gin or vodka and sugar in a large preserving jar with an airtight lid.

• Scrub the orange and dry it well. Tie a long piece of thick string round the orange very tightly so that it cuts into the peel. Hang the orange from the lid of the jar so that it is suspended above the spirit. Cover with tight-fitting lid.

• Put the jar in a warm place and leave to mature for at least 4 months. The orange will gradually shrivel and harden. When it is hard and dry, the faintly coloured liqueur is ready.

Sloe gin

Overall timing
30 minutes plus maturing

Makes 1¾ pints (1 litre)

- 1¼ lb (600 g) Ripe sloes
- 1¾ pints (1 litre) Gin
- ½ Vanilla pod
- 8 oz (225 g) Caster sugar

Wash and dry the sloes well. Prick all over with needle or skewer, then place in wide-necked, airtight jar with the gin, vanilla and sugar. Seal the jar, ensuring that it is airtight, and leave in a warm place for 3 months, shaking the jar once a day if possible.

• Strain the liqueur through muslin and pour into sterilized bottles. Seal tightly. The liqueur can now be drunk but it improves with keeping.

Vanilla liqueur

Overall timing
20 minutes plus maturing

Makes $2\frac{1}{2}$ pints (1.5 litres)

- 1 pint (560 ml) Dark rum
- 3–4 Vanilla pods
- 8 oz (225 g) Brown sugar cubes
- 8 oz (225 g) White sugar cubes
- 1 pint (560 ml) Water

Pour rum into a $2\frac{1}{2}$ pint (1.5 litre) airtight jar. Split and chop vanilla pods and add to rum. Seal and leave for 1 week.

• Put sugar and water in a large saucepan and bring to boil over a low heat, stirring till sugar is dissolved. Remove from heat and add rum to syrup. Mix well and leave to cool.

• Strain liquid through a fine sieve, then pour into sterilized bottles. Seal and leave for at least 1 month before using.

NON-ALCOHOLIC DRINKS

Lemon and honey cooler

Overall timing 7–10 minutes plus cooling

To serve 6–8

4 Lemons
2 pints (1.1 litres) Water
4 oz (125 g) Runny honey
Ice cubes
Sprigs of mint

Pare the rind from the lemons and put into a pan with the water. Bring to the boil, then remove from heat and stir in the honey and the juice from lemons.

• Put into a bowl, cover and leave to cool.

• Strain into a chilled jug, add ice cubes and garnish with mint.

Banana and honey milk shake

Overall timing
3 minutes

To serve 4
2 Chopped bananas
1½ pints (850 ml) Chilled milk
3 tbsp (3×15 ml) Runny honey

Put the chopped bananas into a blender with the chilled milk and honey.
• Blend until mixture becomes smooth and frothy.
• Pour into 4 tumblers and serve immediately with straws.

Creamy milk shakes

Overall timing
5 minutes

To serve 4

½ pint (300 ml) Fresh, frozen or canned fruit purée (strawberry, raspberry, banana, pineapple, peach)

Caster sugar

2–3 Scoops of vanilla ice cream

½ pint (300 ml) Milk

Sweeten fruit purée to taste. Put into blender with remaining ingredients and blend until thick and frothy. Pour mixture into chilled glasses and serve immediately with straws.

Variations

- Change the flavour of the ice cream – for example, use chocolate or any of the smooth-textured ice creams.

Kiwifruit eggnog

Overall timing
3 minutes

To serve 2

1 Ripe banana
1 Ripe kiwifruit
½ pint (300 ml) Chilled milk
1 Egg
2 tbsp (2×15 ml) Runny honey

Peel and slice the banana and kiwifruit and place in a blender with the chilled milk, egg and runny honey.
• Blend all ingredients together until smooth and frothy.
• Pour into glasses and serve immediately.

Meal-in-a-glass

Overall timing
3 minutes

To serve 2

¾ pint (400 ml) Milk

3fl oz (90 ml) Undiluted frozen orange concentrate

1 Egg

1 tbsp (15 ml) Wheat germ

1 tbsp (15 ml) Lecithin granules

2 tbsp (2×15 ml) Honey

Cinnamon or grated nutmeg

Put the milk, frozen orange concentrate and egg into a blender. Add the wheat germ, lecithin and honey.

• Blend ingredients together until smooth and frothy.

• Pour into glasses and serve with a pinch of cinnamon or nutmeg.

Banana health flip

Overall timing
3 minutes

To serve 2

- 3/4 pint (400 ml) Milk
- 1 tbsp (15 ml) Wheat germ
- 2 tbsp (2×15 ml) Lecithin granules
- 3 tbsp (3×15 ml) Peanut butter
- 1/2 teasp (2.5 ml) Vanilla essence
- 2 Bananas
- Flaked almonds

Put the milk, wheat germ and lecithin into a blender. Add the peanut butter, vanilla essence and sliced bananas.
• Blend ingredients together until smooth.
• Pour into glasses and serve, sprinkled with flaked almonds.

Fresh lemonade

Overall timing 15 minutes plus chilling

Makes $2\frac{1}{2}$ pints (1.5 litres)

4 Lemons
8 oz (225 g) Sugar
2 pints (1.1 litres) Water

Using a potato peeler or sharp knife, pare the rind from the lemons. Squeeze out the juice and reserve. Put rind in large saucepan with sugar and water.

• Heat the syrup, stirring occasionally, until the sugar is dissolved. Bring to boil and remove from heat. Add the lemon juice, cover and allow to cool.

• Strain lemonade into a jug, add ice if liked, and serve immediately.

Blender lemon drink

Overall timing
5 minutes

Makes about 2 pints (1.1 litres)

- 2 Thin-skinned lemons
- 3 tbsp (3×15 ml) Caster sugar
- 1 pint (560 ml) Water
- 1 Egg
- 4 Ice cubes
- Mint sprigs

Wipe lemons, cut into pieces and place in blender. Add the sugar and water and blend for 30 seconds or until the lemons are finely chopped.

- Wash the egg and add, whole, to the blender with the ice cubes. Replace the lid and blend for a further 30 seconds.
- Strain into a jug or glasses, add ice if liked and decorate with mint sprigs.

Lemon barley water

Overall timing 2 hours

Makes about 2 pints (1.1 litres)

2 Lemons
$2\frac{3}{4}$ pints (1.6 litres) Water
1 oz (25 g) Pearl barley
4 tbsp (4×15 ml) Caster sugar

Thinly pare the rind from the lemons. Squeeze juice and reserve. Put rind in a pan with $1\frac{3}{4}$ pints (1 litre) of the water and pearl barley.

• Bring to the boil and simmer, covered, for $1\frac{1}{2}$ hours. Strain and discard barley and rind.

• In another saucepan, put the remaining water, sugar and lemon juice. Stir over a low heat until sugar dissolves.

• Add strained barley liquor, allow to cool. Pour into bottles, seal and chill.

• Serve 2 parts Lemon barley water to 1 part lemonade with ice.

Shape-saver lime juice

Overall timing
2 minutes

To serve 1

1 Lime
Crushed ice
Calorie-free tonic water or ginger ale

Cut off a slice from lime and reserve for garnish. Squeeze the juice from rest of lime and put into a tall glass.

• Fill glass with crushed ice and top up with chilled tonic water or ginger ale. Stir and garnish glass with the reserved slice of lime.

Lime milk shake

Overall timing
3 minutes

To serve 4

¾ pint (400 ml) Chilled milk
3 tbsp (3×15 ml) Lime cordial
2 Scoops of lime or vanilla ice cream
1 oz (25 g) Caster sugar

In a blender, put the chilled milk, lime cordial, ice cream and caster sugar.

• Blend the ingredients together till smooth and fluffy then pour into chilled glasses and serve immediately with straws.

Minted chocolate milk

Overall timing 15 minutes plus cooling

To serve 4

1 pint (560 ml) Milk
6 Sprigs of mint
3 tbsp (3×15 ml) Caster sugar
3 tbsp (3×15 ml) Drinking chocolate powder
Whipped cream

Place the milk in a saucepan with 2 mint sprigs and bring to the boil. Remove from the heat, cover and leave to infuse for 5 minutes.

• Discard the mint and stir in the sugar until dissolved. Leave to cool.

• Pour the milk into a blender with chocolate powder and process until frothy. Pour into 4 glasses over ice cubes and top each with a swirl of cream. Garnish with the remaining mint.

Iced grapefruit and mint tea

Overall timing 5 minutes plus cooling

To serve 4

2 teasp (2×5 ml) Tea leaves
2 teasp (2×5 ml) Chopped fresh mint
Sugar to taste
1 pint (560 ml) Boiling water
1 Small can of grapefruit juice
Ice cubes

Place the tea leaves, chopped mint and sugar to taste in a large bowl. Pour over the boiling water and stir till sugar dissolves.

• Leave to infuse for 5 minutes, then strain into a jug and leave until completely cold.

• Add the can of grapefruit juice, then taste and add more sugar if liked. Serve in 4 tall glasses with ice.

Moroccan mint tea

Overall timing
7 minutes

To serve 6

4 teasp (4×5 ml) Green tea leaves
4 Sprigs fresh mint
4 oz (125 g) Caster sugar
1½ pints (850 ml) Boiling water
Sugar to taste

Pour a little boiling water over the green tea leaves in a tea pot. Swirl round and pour out the water, leaving tea in pot.

• Add the fresh mint and caster sugar. Pour over the boiling water and leave to infuse for 5 minutes. Add sugar to taste and serve in glasses.

Teetotal tropical fruit cup

Overall timing
5 minutes plus chilling

To serve 6–8

4 Passionfruit
1 Orange
1 pint (560 ml) Orange juice
½ pint (300 ml) Pineapple juice
1¾ pint (1 litre) Bottle of chilled lemonade
Crushed ice

Scoop out the pulp from the passionfruit, wash and finely slice the orange. Place fruit in a punch bowl with the orange and pineapple juice. Cover and chill for 1 hour.

• Just before serving stir in the lemonade. Ladle into tall glasses containing crushed ice.

Berry fruit crush

Overall timing
5 minutes

To serve 2

8 oz (225 g) Hulled, fresh strawberries
1 pint (560 ml) Grapefruit juice
4 Scoops vanilla ice cream

Reserve 2 strawberries for decoration and put the remainder into a blender with the grapefruit juice and ice cream. Blend ingredients together until smooth and foamy.

• Pour into 2 tall glasses. Pierce a hole through the remaining strawberries, thread straws through and add 1 to each glass. Serve immediately.

10
15

COFFEES

Arabian coffee

Overall timing
15 minutes

To serve 4

4	Small cardamom pods
½ pint (300 ml)	Water
4 tbsp (4×15 ml)	Freshly-ground coffee or
2 tbsp (2×15 ml)	Instant coffee
	Sugar (optional)

Warm the coffee pot if using. Crush cardamom pods to release the seeds.

• Put the water, coffee and sugar if used in a saucepan. Bring to boil. As soon as a froth starts to rise, take pan off the heat and stir. Return to heat, add cardamom and heat until frothy.

• At once take the pan off the heat and pour the piping hot coffee immediately into tiny coffee cups. The grounds and cardamom seeds will settle at the bottom.

Café Brûlot

Overall timing
5–7 minutes

To serve 4

2–4 tbsp (2–4×15 ml) Brandy
3 Sugar lumps
4 Cloves
½ Cinnamon stick
1 pint (560 ml) Freshly-made black coffee
Whipped cream

Put the brandy to taste in a small pan and heat just enough to warm it. Pour at once over the sugar lumps, cloves and cinnamon in a chafing dish, saucepan or heat-resistant jug.
• Set alight and stir for 2 minutes. Pour in the freshly-made black coffee stirring all the time, then strain into tiny coffee cups and top with whipped cream.

Turkish coffee

Overall timing
25 minutes

To serve 4

¾ pint (400 ml) Water
8 tbsp (8×15 ml) Caster sugar or to taste
8 tbsp (8×15 ml) Very finely-ground coffee

Put water and sugar in a saucepan or ibrik and bring slowly to the boil. Remove from heat, stir in coffee and return pan to the heat.

- When a frothy scum forms on top, take pan or ibrik off heat and allow froth to subside. Repeat this process 3 times.
- As soon as the grounds have settled on top, while still hot, pour a little of the froth into the cups. Pour in the coffee so the froth rises to the surface. Add a drop of cold water to each cup to settle the grounds at the bottom.

Irish coffee

Overall timing
5 minutes

To serve 4

8 teasp (8×5 ml) Brown sugar crystals
1 pint (560 ml) Freshly-made black coffee
8 tbsp (8×15 ml) Irish whiskey
4 tbsp (4×15 ml) Lightly whipped double cream

Put 2 teasp (2×5 ml) sugar in each glass. Pour in a little of the hot coffee, over the back of a metal spoon. Stir in 2 tbsp (2×15 ml) Irish whiskey into each glass.
• Top up glasses with coffee to within 1 inch (2.5cm) of rim. Place 1 tbsp (15 ml) cream on top and serve at once.

• Variation
• Pour double cream gently over the back of a dessert spoon on to the hot coffee. The cream then floats on top.

Austrian coffee

Overall timing
5 minutes

To serve 4

1½ pints (850 ml) Hot black coffee
Sugar to taste
¼ pint (150 ml) Carton of double cream
Instant coffee powder

Fill 4 tall, heat-resistant glasses with hot black coffee, pouring it in over a metal spoon. Add sugar to taste.

• Stiffly whip the cream and place spoonfuls on top of coffee. Sprinkle each one with a little instant coffee powder. Serve immediately.

Latin-American coffee

Overall timing
10 minutes

To serve 4

- 2 oz (50 g) Plain chocolate
- 6fl oz (170 ml) Milk
- 1½ pints (850 ml) Freshly-made strong black coffee
- Sugar to taste
- Whipped cream

Put the chocolate, broken into pieces, and milk into a small pan and heat gently until the chocolate has melted. Whisk until frothy.

• Mix the chocolate milk into the hot coffee. Serve at once with sugar to taste and whipped cream floating on top of each glass.

Café orange

Overall timing
5 minutes

To serve 4

3/4–1 pint (450–560 ml) Hot black coffee
8 Twists of orange peel
8 tbsp (8×15 ml) Brandy or Curaçao
Sugar to taste
Whipped cream

Three-quarters fill 4 small cups with hot black coffee. Add a twist of orange peel and 2 tbsp (2×15 ml) brandy or Curaçao to each.

• Add sugar to taste and float whipped cream on top. Trail a piece of orange peel from each cup to decorate.

Café anglais

Overall timing 5 minutes plus chilling

To serve 4

½ pint (300 ml) Cold strong black coffee
4 teasp (4×5 ml) Caster sugar
4 tbsp (4×15 ml) Cocoa powder
4 tbsp (4×15 ml) Vanilla ice cream
½ pint (300 ml) Cold milk

In a bowl, mix together the cold strong black coffee, caster sugar and cocoa powder.

● Chill in fridge, then add the vanilla ice cream and cold milk. Stir well and serve in tall glasses with straws.

Café noisette

Overall timing
3–4 minutes

To serve 4

¾–1 pint (450–560 ml) Hot black coffee
4 tbsp (4×15 ml) Single cream
4 tbsp (4×15 ml) Kirsch
Sugar to taste

Three-quarters fill 4 small cups with the hot black coffee. Stir in 1 tbsp (15 ml) of single cream to each and the same amount of Kirsch. Pass around a bowl of sugar to taste.

Café capucchino

Overall timing
5 minutes

To serve 4

3/4–1 pint (450–560 ml) Hot black coffee

Sugar to taste

1/4 pint (150 ml) Carton of single cream

Cocoa or ground cinnamon

Three-quarters fill 4 small cups with hot black coffee and add sugar to taste.

• Whisk the single cream in a bowl until frothy. Float cream on top of each cup of coffee and sprinkle with a little cocoa or ground cinnamon.

Café d'amour

Overall timing
5 minutes

To serve 4

¾–1 pint (450–560 ml) Hot black coffee
Cocoa powder
Ground cinnamon
8 teasp (8×5 ml) Orange-flavoured liqueur
Cinnamon sticks

Three-quarters fill 4 small cups with hot black coffee. Add a pinch of cocoa powder and a pinch of ground cinnamon to each.

● Stir in 2 teasp (2×5 ml) of orange-flavoured liqueur and serve with 1–2 cinnamon sticks in each cup.

Café royal

Overall timing
5 minutes

To serve 4

¾–1 pint (450–560 ml) Hot black coffee
Sugar to taste
4 tbsp (4×15 ml) Brandy
Whipped cream (optional)

Half-fill 4 heat-resistant glasses with hot black coffee, pouring it over a metal spoon. Add sugar to taste and stir well. Add 1 tbsp (15 ml) brandy to each. (Remember that brandy adds sweetness, so be sparing with the sugar.) If liked, float whipped cream on top.

INDEX